AF451361

An Inquiry Into Reality

ALSO BY JUSSI NIITTYVIITA

We Were Once Human
A Definition of Transcendence

Seeker of Silences
Contemplations of a Silent Mind

A Year of Stillness
A Journey Into Inner Peace and Awakening

I Forgive You
An Unexpected Key to Awakening

7 Days of Presence
A Course in Inner Peace

The Sound of the Bells
A Story of the End of Suffering

More creations of peace and presence

available at www.jussiniittyviita.com

An Inquiry Into Reality

by Jussi Niittyviita

An Inquiry Into Reality
Copyright © 2022 Jussi Niittyviita
www.jussiniittyviita.com

ISBN 978-952-69751-5-3 (paperback)
ISBN 978-952-69751-6-0 (EPUB)
ISBN 978-952-69751-7-7 (MOBI)

A simple child,

That lightly draws its breath,

And feels its life in every limb,

What should it know of death!

- William Wordsworth

Contents

Introduction

For a long time, I've been fascinated by what we humans commonly call *existence*—the curious happening in which things appear and disappear in ever smaller and greater cycles. This happening that underlies everything is most often overlooked in human lives, especially in modern societies that thrive on ideas of growth, advancement, and continuity. I find it highly peculiar why so few of us ever stop to observe and contemplate our own existence and the nature of beings. The matter is typically disregarded and thought to be reserved for scientists, philosophers, or spiritual seekers. This forces me to ponder that either we're not as advanced as species as we believe or are just confused. I'd place my bets on the latter one.

This book is my humble attempt to describe existing as a human being. I hope to clear up the veil of confusion that might cloud *your* experience of existence.

Before we proceed, I must share some information about myself and this book, so you have some understanding of the perspective that produces the words written on these pages.

I've always been more of a silent, withdrawing, and observant kind rather than active and exuberant. Sometimes, over the years, it's been difficult for me to cope in society with all its sound and fury as well as pressures to conform and be sociable. Vice versa, it must have been challenging for others to cope with such a silent and introverted person as I've frequently proven to be. This doesn't mean I've been problematic somehow. I've learned to play by the rules of human society, often at the expense of my inherent nature. Some hues of suffering have been involved in the process of this learning—nothing unbearable but suffering nonetheless.

A certain yearning for solitude has been a healing factor in my life and also, I believe, the major contributor to the books I've written in the past years. Quite a lot of time has been spent in this lifetime gazing silently at a dance of a crackling fire, the endless vortices in a river, and trees swaying gently in the wind. When I was a small boy, the stars in the sky were a source of mystical marvels for me—so distant and small, and yet, so bright and present. The vast space embracing those shiny little diamonds brought an intangible sensation of awe. Gazing at the nightly sky's endless darkness unveiled the kind of wordless wonder in me that always disappeared when I tried to make sense of it.

As the years accumulated, other things occupied my life, many painfully unnecessary and some delightfully welcomed. At some point, I noticed the magic I'd seen everywhere around me as a small child had entirely disappeared for years. This seems to happen to all human beings at a certain period in their lives. Gradually, the sensations of awe and wonder returned like winter slowly turns to spring and spring makes way for summer. The mystical sensations of the little child had silently transformed into curiosity and inquiry, which have turned into a bunch of books so far. In my writings, I've found myself repeatedly coming back to the same questions that have puzzled philosophers and scientists throughout the ages:

Why is there something instead of nothing?
How and to what degree am I involved in this 'something'?

One could approach these questions in a more common metaphor: What is a leaf to a tree? The leaf might seem separate from the tree, yet it still bears within the essence of the tree. Likewise, the tree still bears the essence of a seed, and so on, until we stumble upon the essence of nothingness. Correspondingly, I am here inquiring into existence as a leaf of existence. How weird and wonderful is that!

Another way of putting these questions is an inquiry that spontaneously arose one day while strolling in Lapland's wintery forests with my dog:

How did I end up here?

This question expected no idea of causality as an answer. It had nothing to do with the past or future, where I came from, and where I'm going. Instead, it dived right into the heart of the present moment. I know from intimate experience that the present moment is the closest approximation of reality there can ever be. As this simple question appeared in my mind, I knew I would write a book aiming to contemplate the nature of reality.

The two fundamental questions, *'Why is there something instead of nothing, and how am I involved in this something?'*, can be easily turned into philosophical and scientific principles, arguments, and assumptions. However, that is not the core of my inquiry. My curiosity is placed in the very *experience* of where these questions point. Of course, when writing this text, I can't entirely avoid speaking philosophy and science because the words I write are expressions of the accumulated knowledge that exists in me—the sum total of the wonder of a little boy and a mind of an engineer.

This is in no way a book you should read in hopes of finding any truth or salvation. Instead, these pages encourage you to commence *your own inquiry into reality,* which will potentially shake you awake from a dream. Now, here's a clear breakpoint of this book. You might stop and ask: "What dream?"

If, after some contemplation, you're still oblivious to why you should awaken from any kind of a dream you don't know you're having, then you should stop reading this book. You're probably not yet ready to accept the words that follow from here on. Proceeding deeper into these pages would most probably lead you to a state of intellectual arrogance. We would only end up in an awkward situation where I'm holding the key to *my* home, and *you* are trying to prevent me from opening the door. You have my sincerest blessing to continue if you can accept there's at least some underlying wisdom hidden in the question "What dream?" and therefore, reality might not be how you've always assumed it was.

Now, let me walk you through the contents of this book. I must mention that this is a very surprising situation for me. Even though over 800 pages have come into existence through these hands, in five different books and one course—which all aim to support your self-realization—this is the first time I begin with a gross outline of what I'm going to create. Yet, the exact words that will appear are just as fresh for me as they are for you.

The first chapters, *Paradise Lost* and *The Hall of Mirrors*, start the inquiry into reality by describing the two fundamental obstacles to finding any kind of reality. This is mandatory since we're dealing with units of existence known as human beings. Some deep-rooted mindset mistakes must be corrected before diving deeper into our inquiry. The first mistake is the underlying experience of separation, which governs most human lives today—the sense of an "I, a stranger and afraid, in a world I never made," as put in the poem The Laws of God, The Laws of Man by A.E. Housman. The second fundamental mistake is the evident misuse of the tremendous creative capability of the human mind—something that I call *a false sense of self*. These two mistakes go hand in hand but must be examined separately to make space for any practical realization.

The two middle chapters, *Absolute and Relative Realities* and *The Search for Unity*, further investigate an inherent desire for wholeness that most human beings harbor deep within. This desire springs from the two mistakes addressed above, which often fuel our sensations of alienation and uncertainty. Some people feel these downsides of life more strongly than others. It doesn't matter how it's in your case—the mechanisms are the same in everyone. A false sense of self operates in every single human mind. This is the second break point of this book where you should consider whether or not this book is for you. If you know without a doubt who you are, believe that you have no ego whatsoever, and feel that the two foundational mistakes described above—the experience of separation and a false sense of self—do not apply to you, then I suggest you put this book aside. Consider letting time impose some more suffering on you. Maybe then, after some months or years, you'll find this book's message again either in this book or some other experience in life. Maybe then, you'll be more earnest about accepting it.

The last two chapters, *Rivers of Existence* and *The First and Last Reality*, hold the possibility for a correction of your perception of reality. You'll find no how-to's there, at least not written intentionally. This book is not intended to be a guidebook of any kind. Instead, I present the possibility of realizing something that will change everything. If I were to show you a set of how-to's and write this as a great spiritual teacher who would guide you to your salvation, I would be like a burglar who stormed into your house in the middle of the night. I would steal what is most precious to you. Then, the next day, I would come and give that thing back to you. This sort of false benevolence is not my aim here. So, don't expect intellectual or emotional gratification from this book. Instead, seek to realize the message I share so you'll feel it in your bones.

If any good will result from writing this book, I hope it will encourage you to take a closer look at existence and begin your own inquiry into reality. I don't *need* you to do that, but if you do, I'd be most delighted! I've decided to write this book for *'you'* as the reader for easier communication. Yet, the pages here unfold primarily for *'me'* as the writer. So, don't be offended personally by anything written on these pages. Don't resist with your almighty intellect and knowledge, but try to realize this humble inquiry into reality.

In the name of sincerity, I must confess something before we proceed to the inquiry: writing this book is a mission impossible. This small piece of literature you hold in your hands is my attempt to convey through words something that cannot be conveyed through words. The situation is like trying to describe a clear blue sky to a blind person or explain a beautiful song of a bird to someone who's been deaf since birth. How is that even possible? I sincerely don't know.

Why do I bother to write this at all, then? The answer to this question is likewise a question: Why does a bird sing or a river flow? From this peculiar starting point, I begin my inquiry.

Jussi Niittyviita
25th of March, 2022
Oulu, Finland

Paradise Lost

When you really look at life, it appears like a dream. Sometimes, you feel like you're directing the show, and at other times everything seems highly random and out of control. After some sincere investigation, you quickly discover you know very little about life—why things happen as they do and what purpose the happenings ultimately bear. Digging into the roots of causes and effects will quickly lead to intellectual dead-ends, pointing beyond the outskirts of your knowledge. You don't know *why you are here* instead of the other option, whatever that is.

Many people can indeed present some facts based on science and other beliefs on how everything has come to pass. Yet, being true to yourself reveals that intelligence and rational explanations cannot give you *experiential* knowledge about any kind of reality. Only some indirect clues—grains of knowledge—are scattered on the forest paths of existence, pointing to something utterly unknown.

You have no memories from the time before you popped into this world. The idea of death looming somewhere ahead is as thoroughly unknown as your birth is. Whatever happens between those two great unknowns always seems to be anchored in one single phenomenon: *the present moment.* At one present moment, your young eyes look forward to a life yet to be lived. At another present moment, your weary gaze finds mostly a life already lived. Even though you'd love to argue that *time* separates those two points of view, a quick reality check reveals there's no direct experience of the past you've crossed or the future you'll step into. They are just hazy memories and expectations. The present moment is something utterly inevitable wherever and whenever you are. You cannot exist anywhere else.

Another aspect of this dream-like experience called *life* seems highly obvious also. All material, mental, and spiritual efforts seem to be about escaping from suffering. This often subconscious crusade to fend off suffering appears to be the main reason you so easily drift out of the present moment into a personal interpretation of time. So, my inquiry into reality must begin with the mechanics of this crusade. Suffering as a topic is not always the most gratifying to write and read about, yet it's profoundly necessary.

Most human life today seems to be spent trying to become someone, achieve something, acquire things, or cling to the things already acquired. Sometimes this search for material or spiritual well-being is entirely justifiable to prevent the great pain of suffering from spilling over. It's natural to try to meet the basic human needs of proper nutrition, a fundamental feeling of safety, and healthy social interaction. However, this search for well-being easily becomes too focused on the principle of *more*.

There doesn't seem to be enough growth, wealth, power, success, fame, or whatever enhances our feeling of "having made it" in life. Counterintuitively, "making it" in life doesn't seem to add as much happiness to the human equation as expected. Many achievements do not bring the ultimate fulfillment we so eagerly search for. Our modern oases of well-being might turn out to be rainbows' ends, full of promises and empty of contentment. While chasing the gold that doesn't exist, it's unquestionable that there's a deep calling within us all for a certain kind of wisdom and stillness. We want to act wisely. We want to be at peace. We want what's good for us and the planet.

Almost two hundred years ago, Charles Dickens wrote the famous literary masterpiece *A Christmas Carol*. Before fading away, the Ghost of Christmas Present, the second of the three spirits appearing to the protagonist Ebenezer Scrooge, reveals something that is as essential today as ever. He briefly introduces Scrooge to Man's Children: "This boy is *ignorance*. This girl is *want*." The spirit tells Scrooge to beware of them both, especially the boy, for "on his brow I see that written which is Doom, unless the writing be erased."

I see the boy as a counterpart of the wise actions we pursue and the girl of peace we yearn for. Despite our pursuits and yearning, ignorance and want seem to devour a considerable part of our awareness, hence their name Man's Children. I wouldn't go so far as to call anyone ignorant or wanting because I see the essence of Man as something more profound. *You* can't be ignorant, even though you can plunge into ignorance. *You* can't be wanting, even though you often want things. To put this in other words:

> Who you *think* you are is ignorance.
> Who *you are* is wisdom.
> What you *think* you need is want.
> What *you are* is stillness.

Curiously, ignorance and want are so small a part of our being that they're practically non-existent when really searched for. Our cherished ability to think gives them life, yet their nature is as fleeting as thoughts'. Can you find a thought when you really look for one? If you stop to consciously wait for your next thought, how long do you have to wait? In this light of awareness, thoughts rarely arise. Ignorance and want recede by themselves. The ominous writing on the boy's brow is erased. Of course, this sounds beautiful and promising, yet normally, thoughts can be very persistent in their arising. So, we must dive deeper into this line of investigation.

Way too many expressions of Man's Children—the murmurs of the human heart—exist to deal with in a short book like this. I must approach my inquiry into reality with an even more abstract analogy, one single phenomenon with ten thousand faces that fuels all sorts of confusion. This glass ceiling must be broken before anything close to reality can come through. I call this glass ceiling *a paradise lost*.

Many of our religions and folklore convey a common idea of a primordial earthly or heavenly paradise in which sentient beings were exceptionally happy and delightful. Then, in one way or another, human beings suffered the fate of Adam and Eve and were exiled from this paradise. Other prevailing ideas tell of a certain kind of golden age at the beginning of each cycle of human existence, going round and round, like a Ferris wheel in the amusement park of existence. Some stories describe a paradise inhabited by gods who created human beings either deliberately to express their powers of creation or as an irresponsible accident after some heavy drinking and celebrating.

The idea of paradise is almost always something left behind in the dawn of existence once and for all. It might be something acquirable in the afterlife or sometimes a cyclical one that passes time after time. Be it one way or another, your present experience of life implies that you are not there anymore. Instead of a paradise, you're subject to all kinds of sufferings. From the painful moment when your mother pushed you into the world to the painful moment when your body and brain cease functioning, all sorts of painful moments take place.

I don't mean to be pessimistic—life certainly holds love and all kinds of pleasures as well, many of which seem to make life worth living. Yet, the idea of the primordial paradise *never* includes painful moments. Life was or will be perfect there. No matter how glamorous and beautiful your life "here on Earth" is, it can never sincerely be considered perfect.

All human beings seem to yearn for paradise lost. Who of us doesn't strive for a good life blossoming with morally acceptable pleasures? Can you think of anyone who would not avoid suffering and pain when possible? Most, if not all, of your actions, are governed by a vague remembrance of a life of perfection:

> *There was a time when meadow, grove, and stream,*
> *The earth, and every common sight,*
> *To me did seem*
> *Apparelled in celestial light,*
> *The glory and the freshness of a dream.*
> *It is not now as it hath been of yore;*
> *Turn wheresoe'er I may,*
> *By night or day,*
> *The things which I have seen I now can see no more.*

William Wordsworth describes the most profound conflict of human life in his poem Intimations of Immortality. *There once was a time and place where everything was painless and filled with magic and wonder.* I can't help but think that this lost paradise we all try to regain in most ambiguous ways—for example, eating and drinking in excess, seeking to couple with a perfect partner, expressing ourselves on social media, succeeding in terms of money and fame, trying to become ideal images ourselves—is a product of a sense of separation. It derives from an inconspicuous sensation that the umbilical cord between you and your paradise is cut for good.

Now, imagine you lived in a place of soothing unity, where you didn't have to think about right or wrong. In this place, there's a particular tree: a tree of the knowledge of good and evil. This tree bursts with juicy and delicious fruits you must not eat. They are strictly forbidden! Maybe some deity has told you so, or you just feel it in your guts. Ultimately, the temptation grows too much to bear.

What do you think happens to the blissful 'you' when you taste the fruit of the tree of the knowledge of good and evil? The bliss of *not knowing* explodes in a big bang into knowing that one coin has two sides. Otherwise, it wouldn't be a coin! Knowing this, a primordial sense of unity withdraws, and a profound sense of separation arises in your mind. You instantly realize that something else must be evil if something is good. This implies that you can have the knowledge of good only through evil. Maybe a more suitable name for the tree in Adam and Eve's story would be 'the tree of the knowledge of good *by* evil.'

I find an interesting aspect in this story that I've never heard anyone actually ponder, at least not aloud. When you gain the knowledge of good by evil by doing something you should not do, you don't only gain the knowledge, but *you yourself* are turned into good or evil. You are cast from blissful perfection into imperfection. And why? You counteracted the instructions of the deity or the feeling in your guts. In other words, *you did wrong*. There must have been the right choice also! So, you spend the rest of your earthly life seeking the right choice, trying to fulfill yourself and regain your personal paradise lost.

The idea of primordial paradise before the birth of separation cannot be thoroughly discussed without drawing in also the other side of life. Death is the ultimate limit of your sight, the horizon of your precious knowledge. Maybe this is why it's so often connected to the idea of paradise—death is the threshold where your knowledge of good by evil must disappear again. Quite much every religion and spiritual tradition holds ideas of an afterlife. You've had little choice but to grow into those ideas, just like you've grown into every single idea of your parents and predecessors. You either accept or resist those ideas. Whether you're religious or an atheist, some idea of an afterlife definitely lingers in the back of your skull. It might be a life eternal, a vision of nothingness, or something in between. Afterlife is so big an idea, usually infinite and eternal that you indeed must prepare for it. How do you prepare for an afterlife, then?

Say you're a stone-cold atheist and don't believe in any idea of an afterlife. Maybe you haste to do things, hoard experiences, or acquire stuff because you think you have *only this life* and afterward nothing. Perhaps you find fulfillment from a mindset of anarchy, declaring that "nothing matters," all the while resisting the idea of an afterlife, entangled in the idea without even knowing it. Say you're religious to the bone and follow some of the many prevailing beliefs that instruct you must do right and avoid wrong. Then, if the goddess of good luck smiles upon you, you will be justly judged. You better do things the right way! What would be more terrible than the certainty that your personal paradise was lost forever, that *you* would never be fulfilled? So, you *must* do things the right way.

In fear of the unknown, many massive movements of rigid moral codes and encouragement of "right" activity have arisen throughout the ages. These movements govern much of your actions and decisions today. After all, actions are primarily committed in the personal understanding of right and wrong, of good by evil. Yet, how do you even know what is inherently right or wrong? How do you truly tell apart good from evil when all ideas are good or evil only in relation to each other? All you have is knowledge of the ages stuffed into your head and a set of confusing emotions that you've been taught to cherish through this knowledge.

Then comes the inevitable big question that has puzzled us all from the first sparks of consciousness: Is there an afterlife, really? What happens after life? What is death?

If you wholeheartedly contemplate the question and start being sincere with your experience *here and now*, you must admit that you don't know. So far, your personal experience is *only* life and happenings within life—never after life. So, a better question would be, "What should life know of death?"

You truly don't know what death is and ultimately don't even know what life is. Maybe you believe death includes some heaven or hell in which immense pleasures or sufferings occur. Yet, what is pleasure or suffering when your bodily functions have ceased altogether? Suppose the neurons in the brain no more fire away and form their endless internal connections. What could pleasure or suffering be, then? Maybe you believe there's deep blackness and emptiness after death, in which you float away eternally. Yet, what is blackness without the eyes or emptiness without thoughts? Where are *you* in all these ideas of the afterlife? Certainly not in the body and not in the mind. What, then, is death? It's the end of your knowledge, the great unseen and unknown, which already existed before your so-called birth. You emerged from this unseen and unknown, and evidently, keep emerging. Not cyclically, but continuously. Here and now.

Luckily, my inquiry in this book is foundationally not a question of life and death, even though the subject is crucial as a springboard in the beginning. I don't know enough about them to write even a short book. I also know that you don't know enough about them to understand anything of real value, even if you thought so. So, we're on the same line here. After all, this is an inquiry into *reality*, not ephemeral happenings that rise and fall like waves in the ocean.

What does all this talk about paradise lost, life, and death have to do with reality? Why is it important? Let's hypothesize that who you *think* you are is the sum total of an endless amount of paradises lost—the yearning for fulfillment of all those who have come and gone before you. Who you *believe* to be is dictated by all those ideas of fulfillment waving back and forth in the ocean of humanity. What you automatically do and how you behave are governed by all those pre-written moral codes of right and wrong. Those moral codes create a long list of subconscious dos and don'ts, in other words, your behavioral patterns, that must be met during your life and before your death. Oh, this seems not a hypothesis after all, but an observation! You're still roaming the planet loaded with the nutrients of the delicious fruits in Adam and Eve's story—the knowledge of good by evil.

Is it difficult to accept that you're not in so much control of your life as you thought you were? That you are not 'you' but a still-in-development product of all those who have come before you? Think of a situation. You've dressed in the same style of clothes for the past ten years—all black and relaxed shirts and occasionally something grey to put on, deep blue tapered jeans, and a couple of comfortable sneakers. Then, someone forces you to dress differently, introducing you to all kinds of flashy colors, tight pink shirts, and a pair of brown loafers to put on your feet. "That's not who I am! What will people think of me now!?" you scream in panic.

How do you know who you are? Who has told you who you are? How do people know what to think about you? The uncomfortable feeling you get in dressing differently is your idea of yourself in disguise. Why do you wear specific shoes, buy particular eyeglasses, or go about with a certain hairstyle? You're trying to fend off wrong and cling to what's right. You seek to become someone who'll get you even an inch closer to your paradise lost. Your beliefs and opinions of yourself, others, and the world are the clothes you wear in a righteous mindset. Now, how did you find your own style in the first place? It's quite evident that your style has been around for hundreds or even thousands of years before you. Someone else created it for you, and at the same time, created a paradise lost for you.

So, paradise is lost, and you try to regain it with wearing righteous ideas and deeds. When, then, is paradise regained if lost in the past? Imagine a group of primitive humans gathering together late in the evening under the starry sky. The darkness and silence of the savanna's night are impenetrable. The atmosphere is relaxed—there's still enough food to eat, and no lions were seen during the past day. The smallest children have fallen asleep, curled close to their mothers' warmth. Everything is peaceful. Then, a young man stands up, looks deep into the surrounding darkness, and shortly exclaims: "Tomorrow, at daybreak, we'll go hunting."

When observing human lives today, I can't help but conclude that our paradise was lost when the first of our ancestors thought that one simple word: *tomorrow*. Time plays such a massive part in the way humanity operates today. There are clocks, calendars, and gadgets, but rarely enough time. Reflections of time become reflections of your identity, which you forcefully try to control to maintain a clear picture of who you are. Your life easily becomes an effort in making a sharp-tipped pencil stand on a table—you need constant reassurance and control, or otherwise, the pencil will fall. You might not put it in these exact same words, but if you really look into who you *think* you are, you'll find much truth in these words.

Human lives seem to be expressions of paradises lost, the lost sensation of unity, which is replaced by a profound sense of separation. In the next chapter, I will further investigate the sense of separation to have a more fertile ground for approaching reality.

The Hall of Mirrors

L et's time travel and go back to when you were born just seconds ago. Some nurses and a doctor are present, as well as your mother and father. You're screaming, which is a sign of a healthy newcomer. The doctor cuts the umbilical cord, takes quick measurements of your little body, and places you on your mother's chest. After the pain of physical separation, everything is now peaceful and quiet. Love and relief are in the air.

Now, take a good look at yourself. Who are you, lying there in your mother's warm embrace? You don't know your name. No one has called you by any name yet. There's not even the slightest understanding that you are *something*—a being, a human, or even a baby. At best, the doctor has made some distinct measurements, but that's hardly a definition for who you are. Maybe your parents know something! You hear their voices, mainly your mother's, but they are just voices. Nothing too loud and all soothing. Nothing matters but the warm safety of your mother's closeness, her heart beating against your ear, and the tranquil sounds of her breathing.

What you don't know lying there in an ocean of love and caring is that your parents, the doctor, and the nurses have agreed about a certain matter. "This newcomer can be described in so many ways," they ponder together. "We must have something easy, something explicit to define it. Since we're dealing with only abstract symbols in our language, why don't we create a symbol for this one too." While *you* still live in a world where names can name no lasting name, and voices are beyond meanings, they have decided what *your name* is! And all that has happened without your conscious involvement.

Two years go by in such a state, where nothing matters and nothing sticks. Everything happens without your conscious interference. While you were learning what human beings naturally learn—crawling on all fours, standing up, walking, and using your body in the most innovative ways—the symbol, which is your name, has secretly spread. Now, a whole lot of people know that symbol. Still, you yourself are totally oblivious that you have a name. You have, of course, learned to respond to your name, but that's just a voice you reflexively react to. That voice is not who you are. Now, who are you if you're already walking and babbling, but not a bearer of any name? You still don't know who you are, so the world is like a vast hall of freely flowing sensory perceptions.

Everything happens within *your* hall. Let's call this inner place *the great hall of awareness*.

Then, something spectacular happens on your second birthday in the heat of a joyous moment. While you're laughing and running like the wind, and your father, who's roaring and playing a bear, is about to catch you, a hint of realization occurs. The particular voice that everyone has repeated for so long, which you've learned to respond to, is actually *you*. You *are* a name! A tiny mirror appears in the great hall of awareness. In this mirror, you're looking at a reflection of yourself. In addition to you, many others see that reflection also—they too know that you are a name. You step into the same agreement with all those people. With this step, your feet get mixed up. You stumble to the floor. A fleeting moment goes by. You stand up again, uttering something meaningless. In a fraction of a second, your father picks you up in his bear-like embrace, absolutely delighted that you didn't stay on the ground weeping but stood up again by yourself.

Now that you understand that you are a name, you also understand that another name has just picked you up in his embrace. The embrace is loving, well-meaning, and precisely what must be at such a moment. At that moment, you learn two things. First, when you stand up again, you are loved. Second, the other name is a lot bigger than you! In fact, most others are way bigger than you. This means you're entirely within their power and influence and, most of all, dependent on them. A wordless puzzle forms in your mind. What must I do to earn their love? How must I behave not to lose this love? Two more mirrors appear, huge ones this time.

Some years go by again. You learn that there are many big influencers that you're dependent on. There are also many like you—small, loud, and lively. With all others you meet, a new mirror appears in the great hall of awareness, which doesn't resemble an actual hall anymore. Instead, it's more like a warehouse full of mirrors of different sizes and shapes. When you look at yourself in one mirror, you see one reflection of yourself. When you look at another, you see another reflection of yourself. Some reflections show you love. Some show you dependency—fear of losing the love.

Then comes a big bang. This is a time when you have to fit in. You learn that the vast network of many others has expectations of you, and they will treat you differently if you don't meet those expectations. You realize you're not worthy of their love if you remain as yourself. You're not enough to be loved as you are. The great hall of awareness you once flowed freely in is now a hall of mirrors with ten thousand reflections obstructing your vision.

Now, something called *time* steps into the picture as you try to find yourself in all those mirrors. A sense of urgency arises. You realize there's very little time between the happenings of your birth and something known as death, even though you don't truly know anything about those two. There's also very little time even between the mornings and evenings. And where do you spend most of that time? You're trying to regain a paradise lost and some vague memory of freedom and fulfillment you had before you learned that you are a name. The echoes of the clarity of the great hall of awareness invite you to step closer moment after another. Yet, you don't know what you should do about it. The sense of urgency forces you to commit actions. So, you actively seek ways to be enough to be loved.

This particular creation story of 'you' is an oversimplified version of what's happening. Often, we must simplify things to the core to realize anything of value. The most essential things in life are always the simplest—often too simple for the mind to understand. A mind astray in the hall of mirrors tends to overcomplicate matters and attach meanings to things that are in no way essential or true. You easily end up in a labyrinth of unnecessary information. There, all sorts of byproducts of life emerge that yearn for fulfillment.

On the one hand, you're exposed to all sorts of unfavorable winds. Strong negative emotions need fulfillment through certain words and behavior. They invite thoughts that keep you awake at night. You might think that you *should not* feel so bad. You try to correct all those negative emotions, eliminate them, or turn them into good ones. Who has taught you that life should blossom only with happiness? Why do you believe you shouldn't have negative feelings? Why not be an adorable little black cloud in the sky when it's time to be so? Your thoughts that whisper, "I don't want to feel this way!" express something within you that longs for fulfillment. How do you know what you want and should feel, looking at only one reflection of yourself in the hall of mirrors?

On the other hand, the winds of the world work in your favor. During times of happiness and pleasure, you certainly feel closer to your paradise lost. The emotions are likewise strong, excluding the fact that they don't usually keep you awake at night. The inherent need to express and present your happiness overflows. Sometimes, it's simply time for celebration. How wonderful is existence at those times!

According to a Buddhist idea, you can be born into a bunch of realms, of which the highest is the realm of gods. The gods living there are utterly free of suffering and adversities. Life is so easy that it truly feels like having regained your paradise lost. Yet, such a realm is ultimately unsatisfying because when no adversities exist, you begin to develop unhealthy attachments. You cling to your pleasures, always looking for one fulfillment after another. Inward poverty silently spreads within you while chasing the richness of outer experiences. Somewhere in the hidden corners of your mind, you start expecting and fearing the end of your precious happiness.

Eventually, when you "die" in the realm of the gods, which in your case means that the exuberant and joyous *you* fades away, some intimations of pain and suffering tend to emerge. If you desperately cling to your heaven, your hell becomes as deep as the heaven was high. There cannot be a high without a low. Such duality applies to all material and spiritual highs and lows. So, rest peacefully assured that whatever you're feeling at this very moment, there's always a time-bound experience presenting you with the exact opposite. How comforting it is to know that your happiness will end someday and your unhappiness will not last forever!

So, you're looking *at* and *for* reflections of yourself in the hall of mirrors, armed with a sense of urgency and yearning to be worthy of love, tossed by both favorable and not-so-favorable winds of the world. Recognizing the situation might be a sign of a healthy level of awareness—some remembrance of the spaciousness of the great hall before it was stuffed with mirrors. Your reflection in one mirror at any given moment is simply a *partial* reflection of your inner spaciousness. In those partial reflections, you see many other partial reflections, hence the basic idea of a hall of mirrors. How could you ever know yourself by looking at all those myriad reflections within one reflection? You'd need to be Sherlock Holmes in brain steroids to understand even a tiny bit of it all.

Knowing who you are standing in the hall of mirrors is practically impossible. You cannot think your way out of there. On the contrary, looking at one reflection of yourself tends to engulf your awareness entirely. You become your reflection without knowing it. This becoming, which I call *the false sense of self*, operates within you, as it does in me and every single human being you encounter. It's a process in the realm of time, or more accurately, it *creates* the realm of time. The false sense of self is like a neural network, connecting reflections of your mirrors, seeking to form something stable and permanent, chasing the echoes of your paradise lost. It holds a huge board describing who you are for everyone to see. "This is me!" it shouts and roars, in some people with majestic exuberance, and in some, with a tiny timid voice. Yet, it operates with the exact same force in everyone. The false sense of self enhances and fortifies symbols of who you are. The initial agreement between your parents and the medical staff—your name—was just the beginning of this story.

The false sense of self continuously picks up what's suitable and dismisses what doesn't fit. It's like wearing those comfortable clothes all your life. If anyone ever tries to introduce new ones to you, suffering will spill over. The false sense of self accepts only what's "right", sometimes extending a bit but mainly reconstructing itself in the self-image it has already formed. This great reconstruction process has myriad manifestations—me, mine, for me, by me, through me, at me, in me, from me. And if you're aware of what's happening, you'll see it has infiltrated practically every thought and emotion. In some people, the process includes *'I'* or *'me'* as distinct words or images, and it's quite evident in their speech and behavior. Still, it often appears as an inconspicuous sensation of *you* being the subject, the doer, the main character, and the protagonist in your thoughts and emotions.

The false sense of self was conceived when the first mirror appeared in the great hall of awareness, when you realized there was you and the other. It was enhanced every time you felt you weren't enough to be loved. It was fortified whenever anyone trespassed within its closed territory. The false sense of self creates the realm of time, seeking to become fulfilled with any new mirror image of yourself. It operates through the principle of *more*, frequently whispering obscure words of *ignorance* and *want*.

The false sense of self is entirely dependent on time. Vice versa, your idea of time cannot exist without it. And just like time, it leaves all kinds of traces to be found, footprints in the soil of existence and dents in the fabric of reality. Yet, when you look for the false sense of self or the time it creates, it's nowhere to be found—as if it doesn't exist at all. This is why I like to add in its name the "false sense of." You cannot find a center for yourself, no matter how much you look—not in the body, not in the mind, and not in the world. All your efforts of dissecting yourself physically, mentally, or spiritually will not reveal where you are. Therefore, can you explicitly define who you are?

If you pay enough sincere attention to the shifting nature of who you *think* you are—the reflections in the hall of mirrors—you'll notice that your self-image is by far the most changing thing in your awareness. Thousands of mirrors invite you to look at a partial reflection of yourself, depending on the situation and the people you interact with. Can there be any reality in such continuous change? This is such an important thing to realize before proceeding with our inquiry into reality that I must elaborate on it a bit more.

Imagine that you've built a house. Your house is beautiful and everything you've dreamed that your own house would look like. You've built it mostly by yourself, with some assistance from others. For example, your parents aided you in setting up the foundations in the beginning. When the construction proceeded, you learned to do much by yourself. So, the house is indeed *your* proud creation. Satisfied, you hum some piece of music whose name you don't recall, yet it always seems to suit any situation.

Every time the wind blows, or it rains, or the sun shines too hot, you withdraw into your house. Often, you check the weather forecast to prepare for the coming changes in weather. It makes no sense to go out if it's going to rain soon! Also, whenever you see someone approaching on the driveway, you withdraw into your house so you can properly welcome them. Eventually, you find yourself lingering inside most of the time. The house needs constant maintenance, and over the years, you decide to close the curtains and keep the windows shut. You feel sufficient with the lights you've installed all by yourself. Also, it's nice to change the furniture's place every once in a while. Maybe you get rid of the old furniture and acquire some new ones. Better ones. More exciting ones. Something that would make your house look and feel a little improved.

After a while, you're so busy inside that you stop opening the door to guests, talking with them only through the closed doors and windows. You're sufficient with your good idea of the people that come by. Sometimes the weather is intense, and at other times quite peaceful. "Luckily," you think, "I already know what all kinds of weathers look like and how to have shelter from them." There's no need to peek outside. And whenever there are no guests or changes in weather, you find yourself humming the same forgotten piece of music you did while building the house. It somehow soothes your being and makes the house feel more like home. Sometimes you even hear the music resonating within the walls. You stop to listen to its peaceful rhythm, but you quickly ignore it as nonsense. "Just tricks of the mind, nothing of value!" you think and go on maintaining your house.

So, *the false sense of you* that you behold as yourself is an escape into a small fortress-like house within the mind. It's an utter denial of reality. The views from that house are non-existent. The doors are bolted, so you can't get out of there by your own decision, some kind of technique or method. A hint of claustrophobia is prone to build within. A tiny speck of suffering appears in your being. You find yourself decorating the walls and rearranging the furniture more often. Yet, if you're lucky, after some years or a lifetime when you realize and accept there's absolutely no way out, you suddenly find yourself outside. The familiar music you've hummed and heard all along is now loud and clear. It was a song by the legendary musician Leonard Cohen: "There's a crack in everything, and that's how the light gets in." Looking at your house from the outside, you see an empty shell full of cracks through which the light goes in.

If you thoroughly contemplate *the false sense of you*—the obscure sensation of an 'I' within the body, thoughts, and emotions—you'll find it as a shell with no one inside. It's just a reflection in a hall of mirrors that disappears in the light of your awareness. The sense of being 'you' has nothing to do with who you are. With this realization, you also discover that you don't actually know who you are or what's going on. Yet, that's fine. You're not alone in this. I don't know what's going on either! No one truly does. All we have is a bunch of separate senses of selves seeking reflections of who they are, trying to fix their own houses they think are somehow deficient or broken, ultimately getting nowhere in their efforts. As I said before, the crusade for paradise lost has ten thousand faces.

At this point, you'd do well to trust my word on the matter: *you were never broken*. Your shell doesn't need fixing. If it ever needed anything, that would be your compassionate awareness and loving presence. In the sweet perfection of all imperfections, wholeness and unity blossom. That's where *you* blossom.

Now, some delusions are hopefully beginning to shatter, so at least some light can get in. With the wings of this light, I can continue my inquiry into reality.

Absolute and Relative Realities

et's time travel again. In the last chapter, we contemplated the creation story of your false sense of self. This time, we go way back by a Cosmic Slingshot into simply creation. We'll deal with nothing of biblical proportions here but something easily understood by a simple human mind—my mind and your mind. You'll see how the creation is not left in the dawn of time, like many of the lost paradises, but is still ongoing. It breathes concurrently in all beginnings, middles, and ends, making it all one. Profound wisdom echoes in the Latin word for the Universe, which derives from two words: unus (one) and versus (to turn, to bend, be changed). So, this existence is curiously and literally "turned into one".

Now, the Cosmic Slingshot bolts you back in time through unimaginably long past aeons. You witness planets and moons disappear in the blink of an eye, solar systems scatter into stardust, and tightly woven galaxies explode back into the glimmering smoothness of space. Eventually, like a sharp and strong inhale, everything that exists withdraws into an impossibly tiny space that disappears in the same instant it is born. You arrive at a state of being that can't be described by words, images, or sounds. It is simultaneously so powerful that it can never not be, yet so fragile that if you even so much as exhaled, it would shatter into an infinity of stardust.

So, we must approach this delicate "situation" in a highly simplified and a bit abstract way. Despite being abstract, this interpretation of creation is the most practical thing in the world. If you're earnestly aware of what I'm going to share in the following pages and apply the awareness to what's happening around you, you'll see the practicality of it.

Now, you witness an emptiness beyond all imagination. A kind of emptiness not touchable by any sensory perception, thought, or emotion. For the convenience of writing, we'll call this emptiness *your* emptiness, even though you don't own it. No one can own it because, in a way, it doesn't even exist. It's simply an emptiness that *is* and *is not* at the same time. Nothing more and nothing less. Nothing in it could be a subject for relative comparison—no darkness because there's no light, no voices because there's no silence, no up because there's no down, not even things because there is no nothing. Everything is utterly, hopelessly, and joyfully absolute.

Suddenly, a spark appears in your emptiness, as if it had eternally been there, hidden in plain awareness. Again, we'll call this spark *your* spark, so we're consistent in writing about this all. Your spark is not a product of space; how could there be space with nothing to compare to. Your spark is not a product of time; how could there be time if there wasn't space for time to exist in. No physical, mental, or even spiritual qualities or attributes can be observed in your spark. You cannot say your spark is "included" in your emptiness because your emptiness is still something unimaginable and entirely beyond comparison. There's nowhere your spark doesn't exist, so it definitely exists *now here*. In a way, your spark shares the same essence with your emptiness—it *is* and *is not* at the same time.

Paradoxically, as time doesn't proceed and nothing happens, your spark divides into two separate parts. Now, something can be said to be *here* and something *there*. Let's not yet call this situation "space" since there are only your *here*, your *there*, and your emptiness which is practically *nowhere*. The connection between here and there is like polar opposites of a magnet, intimately tied together in a wholeness, where one could not exist without the other.

A short investigation of the situation reveals yet another profound paradox. For the process of writing about this, I bestow you the ability to set yourself within your three inseparable parts to look *through* and *as* them. When you peek through here, you can say, "I'm here, and that's there." As you peek through there, all you can say is exactly the same: "I'm here, and that's there." And when you peek through nowhere, all you can say is, "I'm now here." You find something absolute still going on, yet also something entirely relative taking place.

Then, your *here* and your *there* become distant from each other. Something that seems like nothing appears between here and there, stretching and keeping them together like a rubber band. You witness the birth of space, or more literally, spaces. There's space between, space in here, and space over there. Of course, to get across space, time is needed. Separation is now very tangible. You see this separation clearly like you would see a crest and trough of a wave—you witness them being separate from each other, even though one's existence is entirely dependent on the existence of the other.

From the crest's point of view, the whole way seems downhill where the trough is, and looking from the trough, all you see is the way up to the crest. Correspondingly, from a magnet's negative pole, the whole flux seems to lead to the positive pole, and vice versa. So, the space surrounding your *here* belongs *there*. Since there are now spaces, somewhere in between must be a horizon dividing the spaces. This horizon is like an open doorway from one room to another—the rooms are separate, even though the same air flows in both of them.

This means that whatever your point of view is, you see something that is not you. Yet, that something practically swims in your essence since you are also the one looking through there. In this peculiar dance of here and there, your parts and spaces form something turned into one, a Universe.

Of course, it's only reasonable that because your emptiness gave existence to your two sparks, why wouldn't it do so to an infinite amount of your sparks also. However, this Rorschach blot of cosmic scale would be too messy to describe, so we'll conclude that endless spaces, horizons, and relative perspectives also exist. We suffice in saying again that "the crusade for paradise lost has ten thousand faces."

Through it all, your absolute and unimaginable emptiness loans its paradoxical (non-)existence to everything. Like this sheet of paper loans blankness to an image that makes perfect sense yet is so simple that it's easily buried under the noise of myriads of everyday heres and theres.

Hopefully, you now consciously recognize that you are here and something else is there. Yet, whoever is here or there is nowhere to be found when searched for. If you really dived deep into this here and now, you wouldn't have any reason to read scribbles like this anymore but the sheer fun of it. Your problems would be gone. Life would simply happen. What are problems if there's no one regarding them as problems? Could there be problems if you recognized that you stand on the same ground of being with all others? I'm not saying everything would be joyful and painless, for we're not living in the Buddhist realm of gods. All I'm implying is that when the false sense of self disappears, unity and wholeness arise everywhere you look. And who's 'you'? No one in particular, and everyone.

Still, a great pain remains! You seem unable to acquire this kind of experience or prolong it when you have it. No worries, though! This pain is just relative machinery of the mind, your false sense of self whispering about your paradise lost, desperately searching for ways to feel the unity again. It's nothing serious. What is it, really, that seeks to become whole? Who pursues the experience of unity? Can anything *become* whole in a world where everything already *is*? Is it possible to fix something that has never been broken? On this path of inquiry, you need time to realize there's no time. You need others to realize there are no others. You need 'you' to realize there's no 'you'. One joyful paradox after another makes me think of the strange wheel of existence as a cosmic joke—all fresh and new in the beginning, with drops of suffering here and there in the middle, leaving you with only a good laugh in the end.

Now, we have some clues and ideas about reality, but I must confess that I still don't know what's going on. What we just went through with the Cosmic Slingshot is clearly observable everywhere in human experience. Still, it offers only some hints of reality here and there at best—nothing explicit yet. We now recognize that all kinds of sparks appear, creating all kinds of totalities relative to the core. We've also discovered that all those relative things undeniably serve our purpose in our inquiry into reality.

So, what do these abstractions mean in the context of the human experience? Your experience seems to always be *here*, and wherever your focus goes, something else is *there*. Here's you, and there's other. This applies to both animate and inanimate nature, as well as ideas. When you fight for the idea of good, something other must represent evil. In your right, something other has to be wrong. Where you stand for justice, something other stands for injustice. When you're in pain, the yearning to relieve the pain emerges. In your happiness, you hear faint echoes of past unhappiness. Many different worlds exist in this strange play of here and there. It's undeniable that you've tasted the fruit of the tree of the knowledge of good by evil, no matter how symbolic the story might be.

This knowledge gives birth to personal and collective realities, which are always thoroughly relative. Your experience of life might revolve around you—your work, your house, your family, your body, your social activities, your endeavors, and your values. Or you might be centered in a broader perspective—our work, our religion, our family, our success, our nation, our planet, and our actions. Such relative things bear only relative importance, never absolute importance, even though it might often feel like it. Also, relative things can produce only relative truths, which are inherently wobbly and short-lived. Where's the truth in what you think when others think differently? What's the importance of your actions when others act differently? Your perspective shrinks and grows depending on the situation, just as your false sense of self changes from moment to moment. Where do you place yourself? From where do you try to find your realities? Why? These questions aim not to judge and stop what you're doing. Instead, I present them to shed some light of awareness to whatever you're doing.

If you place yourself within any truth—either your truth or our truth—you're speeding in a getaway car of the mind. The chase includes one relative thing trying to flee from another relative thing. You're trying to catch yourself while escaping from yourself. Your cherished opinions and beliefs are born of an innate drive to flee from other opinions and beliefs. In this great getaway, you lose yourself in the heat of what has been and what might be. Whenever you catch yourself from thinking, ask yourself: "Where was I? Was I really present with those thoughts? To whom did those thoughts occur?" Luckily, your getaway car can't outrun the speed of the light of awareness. This awareness anchors you to the present moment and reveals some striking and soothing absences when you're not thinking. For example, the absence of your cherished truths, beliefs, and opinions. And most clearly, the absence of who you *think* you are.

In its innermost essence, the light of awareness is something profoundly vaster than what can be conveyed through words. I once heard a priest refer to it at a funeral while talking about God's nature: "Your voice is not enough to describe it." It's the breath of the absolute, which cannot be conveyed through the relative realities of images and words. This is why, in the introduction chapter, I mentioned this whole book is a mission impossible. Still, the absolute is here and now as your sparks and your emptiness.

The Search for Unity

I once read a fascinating bedtime story with my daughters when they were younger. The protagonist was an elf named Nugget. He had been living very content for a few hundred years in the attic of an old house. Then, one day, he heard a conversation while lounging in the hearth's warmth. Two men downstairs talked about something called "gold". As Nugget listened to their conversation, it became evident that this yellow and shining substance was something that brought happiness to whoever found even a tiny bit of it. Nugget didn't know what gold was or even what happiness was. Still, gathering from the men's behavior, gold seemed so miraculous that he instantly stood up, packed his little backpack, and headed to search for gold.

This gold that was supposed to bring happiness proved to be a difficult thing to find. Nugget roamed across the lands, seeking and trying to find traces of gold. As he arrived on the edges of a vast yellow flower field, he thought it must be gold, for the sweet scent of the field enchanted him to the core. When he sat on a huge rock on the top of a fell after a long day of walking, he thought that the yellow and orange hues in the horizon were gold, for such a beauty they were to his eyes. The gold he didn't find, yet he found many other things on his travels. Things that made his heart pound faster in their beauty, things that made tears pour out from his eyes in their elegance, and things that brought deep peace in his soul after long and hard days of searching.

On his travels, Nugget learned from more men's discussions that gold was often found in creeks and rivers. So, he decided to build a tiny hut near a creek flowing with cool and fresh water. One late autumn morning, when light snowflakes were hovering down from the sky, and the small nearby pond was covered in thin ice, Nugget stumbled upon a small black dog badly mistreated by humans. He took the dog to his tiny hut and healed the wounds with the elves' sempiternal remedies. From that day on, the dog followed Nugget everywhere. Together, they sought gold from the creek soon to be frozen for the long winter, gazed at the beautiful sunsets on top of the fell, and spent peaceful evenings in the warmth of their tiny and cozy hut.

"I've found nothing yellow or shining, yet it seems that I've always felt happiness and peace," Nugget pondered one evening while sitting on a fallen tree trunk with the dog. They watched the creek's clear water run slowly downhill for a short moment of silence. He patted the dog's soft and warm back and whispered. "I had it already while lounging there in the warmth of the hearth. Now it smiles upon me with another face here and now, even though my feet are a bit cold and fingers stiff from all the digging." From that day on, many gold-diggers would see glimpses of an old elf and a small black dog if they paid any attention to Lapland's nature around them. Even though the gold-diggers had found no traces of gold, a strange yet familiar peace and stillness would enfold them. The gold-digging would become an activity among all other activities, with nothing to pursue, yet shining with brilliant and simple joy.

A search for unity, an inherent desire for wholeness, is the most powerful driving force in human lives. It's the obvious yet hidden agenda in all our efforts to find "gold"—the substance or situation that would make us happy and content. Many of us are so obsessed with finding the gold that the hidden agenda remains hopelessly hidden. The gold-digging has become an unconscious habit echoing in most human societies. At a very young age, we learn that wealth, health, and relationships are the basic ingredients of living a proper life. There must always be *more* money and fortune, *more* physical vigor and years to live, and *more* connection and belonging. The great hall of awareness is stuffed with such mirrors, and mostly in those reflections, we commence our gold-digging—our search for unity and hopes for finding a personal paradise lost.

Your search for unity mainly focuses on other human beings, either directly through relationships or indirectly through wealth and health. In them, you try to find your personal fulfillment. You believe that another human being can make you whole. The peculiar part of this search is that the very thing that you most expect to make you whole—other human beings—is the leading cause of depriving you of the experience of wholeness. You might have some temporary experiences of fulfillment on this road. Still, it will soon become evident that your feelings of wholeness are prone to end up in feelings of separation and loss. This is not necessarily a bad thing but the natural course of human life. Separation exists because wholeness exists.

Your search for unity isn't restricted only to human relationships, even though they are a gravitating force. You seek unity from nature also—plants, animals, weather, and places. Simply spending some time in the wilderness can give you a glimpse of unity. The scent of a beautiful flower, the elegant movements of a bird landing on a branch, the majestic play of a thunderstorm, or the serenity of a still forest lake can open the door to quite peaceful states of being. The modern way of efficient and productive living introduces a certain kind of wistfulness, a desire to settle down and lie on green grass in the shade of an old tree or idly stroll on an empty beach doing absolutely nothing but enjoying the warm sand under your bare feet.

The search for unity doesn't end in concrete things like other humans or nature but extends even further.

Where masses of people gather, whether physically or in their shared worldviews, a sensation of belonging tends to blossom. In gatherings, you search for unity from more abstract phenomena, like religions, nationality, money, and maybe even *time*. Time is involved primarily in the expectations of finding your unity. There must surely be something in the future, near or distant, that will make you whole and regain the paradise lost. Something that would reconnect yourself with a primordial peaceful state of being.

Wherever you expect to find unity and wholeness, there's a huge egoic pitfall also. You might think that life is supposed to make you happy and fulfilled. You might believe that your privilege as a human being, a bearer of a higher state of consciousness, is to do things that you think express yourself the best. A beautiful idea, but what's the pitfall? The false sense of self—the house that you built and bolted shut. How on earth could you ever express yourself truthfully when your perception of your own qualities and attributes is blinded by your very ability to perceive? After all, your perception is thoroughly relative. Unity and wholeness have nothing to do with doing or self-expression. Instead, they underlie all doing and expression.

Then comes the big question: how do you know when you find unity? How do you know when you're whole as a being? You just do. You no longer ask questions about what would make you whole or expect something in the future to give you a sense of purpose and belonging.

You recognize you've stopped operating through *a philosophy of as if.*

This particular philosophy was introduced by german philosopher Hans Vaihinger in 1911. "As if" implies that because human beings are incapable of knowing any true reality, we create thoughts and beliefs and then assume they match reality. In other words, we act "as if" reality matches our thoughts and beliefs. We pursue happiness as if happiness was some definite grand goal in life. However, can you directly observe and experience the happiness that appears somewhere in the future? We strive to acquire more money as if money was a necessity for a life of wholeness. Yet, what is a dollar but a sheet of paper or a number in your bank account? We become spiritual seekers as if enlightenment or the grace of god would save us from suffering. What is enlightenment or a god but an idea that stuck to your mind after someone brought it to you? We fall in love as if love was something that would keep us unified until the end of time. Still, is it love or dependency you have in mind? And here comes the best one! We desperately need more time as if time was something that is running out. What is time but an idea you harness in your crusade to become whole?

These things might all be difficult to accept, and I'm not asking or expecting you to accept them here and now. As I said in the introduction of this book, all I'm aiming for is to encourage you to begin your own inquiry into reality. I promise *your inquiry* will give you a more profound sense of unity than any of those ten thousand faces of relative realities and *as ifs*.

Counter-intuitively, a certain kind of solitude seems to precede unity. You don't need escapism or reclusiveness as Jesus and other mystical figures have embraced. You don't need a desert to wander in alone for forty days. Solitude can be here and now even when surrounded by people and society—it's sincere inward awareness devoid of conditions. You simply take a step into your own being and see what's going on inside. In this solitude, you return home and regain an intimate connection with yourself. This reconnection is nothing mystical or spiritual. It's *consciously* experiencing whatever you experience at any given moment. You're the one without whom no experience could take place. Better focus on that one instead of external relativities. Interestingly, when the connection to yourself is re-established, or more accurately put, recognized, a subtle sensation of unity begins to surface.

This sensation is not normally recognized in the mechanical human mind, where you are restricted to the house you've built and wearing the same clothes year after another. The idea of 'you' in control and separate from your surroundings—the false sense of self—creates much distraction and is most probably the biggest of obstacles to any sensation of unity. Only after this obstacle dissolves will you begin to see how birds cannot fly without air, fish cannot swim without water, and you cannot walk without ground. The ground under your feet is just as much in control of your walking as 'you' are. A possibility arises to recognize that the ground of being is the shared ground upon which the whole of existence walks.

Unity is not an experience 'you' gain after long and hard searching. It's not an emotion 'you' have when your paradise lost is regained. The unity I'm referring to includes your search, experiences, and your paradise lost. You won't ever find it, but you look *through* and *as* it, as the naked awareness outside the house you've built. The situation is paradoxical to the core and entirely out of 'your' control.

So, what can you do about it? How do you bring forth unity? You might try to step out of your own way and let grace, or whatever you call the unseen forces of existence, work it out. You might force your unity into being by relentless practices and methods. After you've tried out everything, you'll realize there's *nothing*, very literally, that you can or cannot do to reveal unity. This is the climax of the pain of your search and the time for a great surrender.

After your search crumbles to dust, soon to be blown away by the winds, all that's left is the simple awareness of what's happening. This awareness includes what 'you' as a person are or are not doing. The dust might take some time to clear up, yet it will become evident that there never was *time* to begin with. Unity, the ground of being, was firmly under your feet every step of the way. Inquiring into unity is a symbolic act that many of us commence during our lives—most of us in the moments of our greatest sufferings. In those painful moments, the great surrender seems to become most clearly available.

With your inquiry, you're much like young gold digger Scrooge McDuck in Klondike's White Agony Creek, holding an unusually heavy ball of mud in his hands. He thinks: "Such a huge nugget of gold would make me the richest man in Klondike!" Still, a second before washing the mudball, he ponders: "If I'm correct about this mudball, I've found at last what I've been searching for my whole life. Yet, will anything ever feel the same after this? Will the scent of fresh air be somehow better? Will the sun shine any brighter during my days? Will there be more magic in the starry night sky? Or is that all gone from me forever? Do I really want to become wealthy?" Now, we all know how the story of Uncle Scrooge goes from that point. There's no end to his personal principle of *more*, even though some light occasionally shines through the cracks of his money bin.

With this book, I'm trying to point out how important it is to constantly stay in that very second before washing the mudball in your hands. Pursue relative realities or recognize something much deeper? Maybe stop acting *as if* the mudball was a nugget of happiness and fulfillment, and instead, just look, listen, and feel what's going on around and within you? Of course, you do what you will. Luckily, it's not a must or must not do situation. Reality already shines *in you* and *as you*. All it ever asks from you is earnest awareness, some cracks in the shell of your false sense of self, and spacious openings where the light can come in. You don't do anything about it or leave anything undone because of it. You just consciously let the light come in.

Rivers of Existence

A friend once told me that I must write about mysteries, mansions, heirs, romances, and murder to sell truckloads of books. In a way, I've done exactly that in these pages. Though I highly doubt the popularity of a book like this. We've looked into the house you built yourself, representing the mansion as the main stage of your life's play. We've contemplated the nature of unity and wholeness, which is something that romances usually aim at. What about the heir and murder, then? The heir is your false sense of self, to whom you gave life, and after coming to your senses, compassionately and kindly murdered. Not with your hands or some tools of the trade but simply being aware of it as it is. The mystery lies in the murder, of course. Even though it seems you committed the murder all by yourself, you didn't do it alone. You obviously had help, but from whom? Your self, which is nowhere to be found!

Also, the mystery deepens when you notice that there's no body of a false sense of self lying around. The only logical conclusion is that your false sense of self was never murdered at all because it never existed in the first place. Yet, you can't be entirely sure what happened when thinking about the situation. After following all kinds of traces of reality, you still don't know what's going on. There's no concrete evidence of a murder, even though you can observe an amazing absence of something that was murdered. Any traces of evidence open the door to the unknown. Sometimes mysteries in stories must remain mysteries. Accepting the ultimate unknown will bring great peace, where mysteries are no longer puzzles to be solved but silences to be experienced.

This kind of peace is described curiously by Admiral Richard E. Byrd, who wrote about his expedition to the Antarctic in 1934. "The day was dying, the night being born—but with great peace. Here were the imponderable processes and forces of the cosmos, harmonious and soundless. Harmony, that was it! That was what came out of the silence—a gentle rhythm, the strain of a perfect chord, the music of the spheres, perhaps." Then, Byrd describes how he was a part of that rhythm, and at that moment, there was no doubt of man's oneness with the universe.

Oneness. Unity. Wholeness. It seems there's light even in the darkest and most perilous situations known to man. Luckily, I've not tasted such intense psychological or physical pains so far. I hope I never have to, and I sincerely hope the same for you. The natural inclination toward the paradise lost—a life free of suffering—works in all human beings. Yet, none of us is immune to the woes of the world. At such deepest and darkest moments, inquiring into reality becomes ever more important. Why? Because unconsciously experienced suffering will ultimately spill over and become contagious, leading to all kinds of calamities we've witnessed in the history of humanity and still witness quite regularly.

Why do you expect life to make you happy and painless while trying to suppress suffering? Is life supposed to grant you all the positives without the negatives? Maybe, after a sincere inquiry into reality, you'll find the grace of unity in some river of suffering, no matter how gruesome and furious. Ultimately, that grace is no different from finding unity from a river of pleasure. All rivers, even though they are of different lengths, have different turns, and carry different volumes of water, eventually lead to the ocean.

So, if all rivers—lives, entities, and happenings—are connected to the same ocean, why do they seem separate and not unified? According to our creation story of *here* and *there*, the separation must be, so that unity can be. Together, they are whole. It's about connecting the dots, like in children's puzzle drawings. When the connection is realized, the dots form an image that was always there on the paper. The connection creates the flow of the image. Likewise, a river flowing alone through the lands wouldn't be a river if it wasn't connected to vaster pools of water. It would stagnate after losing connection to something beyond its own length. This connection can produce all sorts of oceanic experiences, but it's not an experience in itself, like a dot on the paper is not much of an experience alone. Still, without all the dots, the child could not draw the image as it is. Every single dot is essential to form the whole picture. Correspondingly, the flow at given point is crucial for a river to be a river, just like *your world* wouldn't exist if *you* didn't exist.

There are many perspectives from which to look at your world. Yet, they can be roughly categorized into two: the perspectives of separation and unity. What perspective would you prefer while dealing with the world? This is not a question of right or wrong but of consciously appreciating whichever you choose.

If you choose the perspective of unity, you have the possibility to observe something immense. I'm saying *the possibility* because, as I wrote earlier, 'you' as a person cannot bring it about. If you make yourself available for this possibility, an experiential understanding arises of how everything is connected. Metaphorically speaking, you see how the course of water goes through vaporizing from the ocean, gathering in clouds, falling down in the rain, closing up in rivers, and flowing into the same ocean again. You observe that rain is water falling downward and vaporization is water falling upward—how gravity as a unifying force makes things heavy and falling, yet at the same time, is the root of lightness. You understand how the same rain gives birth to beautiful roses here as well as troublesome weeds there. The same water drenches both beggars and kings. Everything is so clearly and beautifully connected. This understanding doesn't include knowledge as memory or intellectual capacity. Also, there's nothing spiritual in it, either. It's practical as anything can be. It's nothing more and nothing less than your intimate experience of the present moment.

To elaborate on this more, let's briefly investigate the flipside of unity, the perspective of separation. Imagine that you've drawn a circle on a piece of paper. In separation, you believe the circle is defined solely by the thin line you've drawn. You see a distinct border between the inside of the circle and the outside, which is not the circle. If you stood inside the circle, declaring, "This circle is me!" you would perceive everything outside as not you. The situation resembles a map of the Earth, where we have drawn arbitrary lines to claim lands for ourselves and establish national identities of 'us' and 'not us'. In such a situation, you don't pay sincere attention to the paper on which your circle is drawn. The lands and nature we've divided with lines on a projection don't get the unconditional appreciation they deserve. Awareness is lost in relativity. When someone comes to you with abstract spiritual mumbo-jumbo about something called *a false sense of self* that desperately searches for a paradise lost, you'll resort to the most convincing tool the false sense of self has: denial.

"What false sense of self? I see no false senses of selves around here!" If you don't recognize one within, you're most probably looking through the eyes of the false sense of you—a relative reflection of yourself in the hall of mirrors. You're dwelling inside the little circle you've drawn on the paper, looking at the outside as something separate from you.

As the fulfilling side of the separation, the perspective of unity creates a profound understanding of the absolute. This understanding implies that the little circle on the paper is encircled by everything else. Without everything else, the circle wouldn't be a circle. It can't have an inside without an outside. Therefore, the very essence of the circle is directly defined by what it is as well as everything it is not, which practically means the circle is defined by simply *everything*. Additionally, the understanding of the absolute arises in realizing that the circle and everything else can exist only because of the paper. Without the paper, you can't draw a circle or anything else on a piece of paper. So, the whole existence and its relative parts can only be because of their inherently absolute nature. It's as simple as that.

With the wings of this understanding, the familiar sense of mystery arises beyond the outskirts of your knowledge. Still, this one is a mystery that doesn't need solving. Any attempt to solve it only drives any solution further away. Any thought trying to figure out the mystery leads only deeper into the maze of unnecessary knowledge. Even with this writing here, we're already walking around the maze's outer walls. However, we're not going to step in but observe where the mystery is best observed: the present moment.

Here and now is a shifting reality that has already disappeared when you try to make sense of it. The present moment is like a boat where you sit still, watching the wake of the boat fade and disappear into the ocean. Everything you observe in the wake has reality only in your observation here and now—the past doesn't exist but as a memory occurring in the present moment. Everything you anticipate in the unknown horizons ahead—in the future—is only your conclusions about the wake of the boat. These conclusions have reality only in some hazy and shifting memories occurring in the present moment. This realization is beautifully put into words by a not-so-well-known Finnish poet, Unto Kupiainen, in his poem *The Rower* (which this translation does not nearly do justice):

> *Strange is the flow and strange is the boat,*
> *they do not go by the streams of your dreams.*
> *The evening is in Man, the morning is a mystery;*
> *from evening to morning is Man's journey.*

> *From evening to morning, there's nightly way;*
> *if you have faith, you will not break.*
> *Gazing backwards, you row forwards*
> *a strange boat into strange waters.*

Healing becomes possible in the recognition that you're rowing a truly strange boat into utterly strange waters. "Healing from what?" you might ask. From any sense of separation you might have had along the nightly way. From the experience that you are a small dot surrounded by many other dots, separate from each other on the paper. From the expectation that life must fulfill your dreams and give back your paradise lost. From your precious knowledge, that mostly leads you astray into the maze of unnecessary information. From the past that no longer exists, that so easily lures you into a future that never exists. In this healing, the mysterious morning sheds light on your nightly way. You row forward, blissfully not knowing what's going on. In this peaceful state of not knowing, you cultivate faith. "Faith in what?" Another question pops into your mind. Faith in nothing in particular, yet in everything that *is*.

This all might sound a bit too poetic, so let's examine your strange boat from another angle. Since you were two years old, your body has accumulated much weight and height. All kinds of experiences have come and gone. Some have stuck to you as memories and beliefs. Some hung around for their time until they left you. As a byproduct of all those experiences, your brains are wired in such complicated ways that no one doesn't actually know how they operate, except that the wiring is constantly going on even as you read these words here and now. Your body doesn't have a single cell in it that was there when you were two years old. You've had so many replacement parts over the years—physically, mentally, and spiritually—that the boat you began your nightly journey with has practically none of its original parts. How, therefore, can you ever think or talk about 'I' or define yourself in any definite way? You are as clear an expression as possible for the shifting reality of the present moment. You *think* you know who you are, but nothing beats you in the game of strangeness. And you're rowing forward on a river that shares the same mystery with yours. On that river, some furious rapids present you sufferings, and some peaceful turns flow with pleasures.

In trying to prolong the river to ever greater lengths—to think of yourself as a permanent 'you' who believes to be in control—you become like Sisyphus in Greek mythology. Sisyphus cheated death twice, so the gods sentenced him to roll an immense boulder up a hill. When nearing the top, the boulder was destined to roll back down. Of course, the punishment would last for eternity. I interpret the myth so that the hilltop represents death, which Sisyphus was eager to cheat. When death does not occur as the polar opposite of life, life becomes a gruesome game of rolling a boulder up a hill in vain. Without death, life loses its mystical poetic nature and rhythm. If you cling to 'yourself' as the protagonist of life, you're trying to cheat death. Overpowering suffering will likely emerge. As long as you take credit for your successes or failures and think 'you' are the doer of what you're doing, you swim against the river's flow. You repeatedly roll the boulder up, only to see it fall down again.

What's the reason you're constantly working the boulder upwards? Have you ever paused and looked at what's going on around you? A whole lot of fellow human beings intensely roll their boulders toward their hilltops. A gleam of a paradise lost shines in their eyes, and their halls of mirrors reflect all sorts of false senses of selves. Better yet, most of us shout our opinions to the nearby hills on how others should roll their boulders. Many of us often change their hill because someone else's hill seems more promising. That's still rolling a boulder up a hill. I must clarify here that this is not a judgment toward anyone but simply a compassionate observation.

What if you dropped all effort with your boulder and turned your eyes downward? There, in the great silence, you might see glimpses of a small river running through the hills and mountains. "Tao is like valley streams," Lao Tzu wrote a couple of thousand years ago. Amid all the noise and fury of life, valley streams flow ever onward in silence, nourishing lands, and connecting them to the vast unknown oceans. Even though we recognize the peacefulness of those streams, we don't know what they are. Again, Lao Tzu put it quite simply: "I don't know its name. Call it Tao. For lack of a better word, I call it great. Being great, it flows. It flows far away. Having gone far, it returns." The course of water always leads to a return. In the great silence of valley streams, it is best observed.

Let's investigate something that I call *a Silence Experiment*. The instructions for the experiment are as simple as anything. If you have difficulties understanding it, simply observe a dog or a cat for a while. They are grand masters of this experiment:

While you sit there, you do *not* concentrate on arriving at a particular state of being. The Silence Experiment is *not* a formal meditation because you simply sit there quietly. You do *not* commence some kind of practice or a technique of sitting or breathing. The Silence Experiment is *not* an attempt at mind control. With this list of all the things you're *not* doing, you end up not knowing what you should be doing or what should happen. So, all that's left is to remain aware. A whole lot of things arise in your awareness. Thoughts. Emotions. Bodily sensations. Occasional urges to do something. Temptations to wander in all kinds of expectations and memories. Some irrational restlessness arises in the dead space of the Silence Experiment.

All those things that arise in your empty room are thoroughly relative, rising and falling like waves in an ocean. As you witness all those things appearing and disappearing, you actually witness the roots of all the problems humanity faces, individually and globally. Yet, here, the roots are not the problem itself! Being able to observe them is a sign of a healthy level of awareness and wisdom. Problems emerge when you follow the temptation to grow into all those relative directions. In other words, if you lose your *being* even for a while, you *become* centered in all those relative things.

Becoming centered means gravitational force. What does this mean in your life, then? It's no big secret that most human thinking consists of negative and fear-based ideas—blind yearning for paradise lost. Gravitational force toward such ideas is the cause of turmoil and wars. Is it difficult to accept that the very same mechanisms are at work within your mind and body that have produced—and still produce—the calamities you usually only hear about in history books or the news? Can you find *the idea of yourself* that makes this difficult to accept? How real is this idea of yourself, even if you could find it?

Better to lead a life without a center and flow with the valley streams. This might sound like promises of your paradise lost, yet life without a center is not the way of no suffering. Instead, it's the way of least suffering— compassionately accepting and living through all your sufferings, and consequently, not causing redundant sufferings through your words and actions. Without a center, you become intimate with Man's natural and peaceful nature while journeying from evening to morning—from birth to death. You recognize and accept the strangeness of your vessel and the unknown nature of the waters carrying you.

The First and Last Reality

We've come an interesting way only to find out there's not much to say about the ultimate reality. Anything I write here is only a Zen finger pointing at the moon. If you look at only the finger, you'll miss all the grace and glory of the magnificent night sky. In all our efforts to understand reality, we must admit that we don't know the truth of it. Also, we must acknowledge that there's no explicit center called 'you' or 'I' anywhere, even though it often seems like there is. This makes the whole dance of existence even more strange and unknowable.

Existence is like a soap bubble machine with a never-ending battery. Bubbles appear and disappear, and in all efforts to define who we are, we end up only with a lot of air and empty space. All kinds of shiny colorful patterns can be observed on a bubble's surface. Despite seemingly real, the patterns are just rays of light penetrating and reflecting from the impossibly thin film that seems to be a bubble. This thin film reflects images of the environment and other bubbles. It's tossed by the slightest of winds in unpredictable directions. Eventually, when it bursts and disappears, two things happen.

First, the reflections on the thin film no longer exist because the film doesn't exist anymore. Yet, the very essence of what made up the bubble still exists; the air hasn't disappeared anywhere. The light still embraces everything that remains. Second, once the bubble disappears, its image is no longer reflected on the thin films of the other bubbles. Luckily, new bubbles constantly emerge to give and create new reflections. So, the suffering of losing one reflection is eventually replaced by another— maybe not exactly similar, but just as lovable.

You find stillness and wisdom in recognizing that all those reflections are essentially the same light scattered in beautiful, diverse colors. *Ignorance* and *want* recede by themselves without any effort from you, as if they never existed at all. The principle of *more* no longer operates within you. Luckily, your bubble's thin film doesn't need to burst and disappear to create space for this unity and wholeness. Your paradise is regained by simply recognizing the nature of the soap bubbles, including your own. Then, you realize that *you* shine freely within and without everything. *You* flow as one air inside and outside all those myriad bubbles.

So, where do you locate yourself? In the relative reflections of those impossibly thin films, or the light and air which are absolute in the existence of the soap bubbles? The whole world is located within you when you locate yourself in no particular space or time, a body or identity. The false sense of self will try to fight this, even if you feel it's true. You might ask the location question in another way: How can you objectively locate yourself within anything?

The answer can be approached in many ways. For example, the sun is perceived as a huge shining ball in the sky by day. Yet, where's the sun located at? What's included in the sun? It's not just a distant phenomenon but something that includes you and the whole of Earth. Our planet is embraced by the sun's rays and bathes in its warmth. The sun's radiation in all its wavelengths is not separate from the sun but bears the very essence of it. How about the Earth, then? What's included in it? Rocks and minerals, the atmosphere, water, plant life, animal life, and yes, also human beings. Nothing is separate here on Earth—it's all simply a totality that's included in the sun. What's included in a tree? A tree has roots, a trunk, and leaves. There's water, nutrients, and light doing their cycles within it. So, a tree is an expression of the Earth as well as of the sun. What's included in a human being? A human being has skin, a stomach, lungs, and all sorts of sensory apparatuses. Everything that makes the human being tick expresses the very essence of the Earth. So, a human being is an expression of the trees, the Earth, and the sun. And here's a good one! How about the distant shining stars you witness as tiny specks of light in the blackness of space? The next time you go out in the dead of night and see those little diamonds above, you may recognize how your eyes bathe in their light, being expressions of those distant stars. We can look into ever tinier microscopic realms and vaster celestial bodies and inevitably see how everything is an expression of everything else.

I know this is spelled out with repetition. My point is that defining the exact location of anything is utterly impossible. If you perceive something in any way, it means you're included in that something in all perceivable ways. You witness specious beginnings and endings, borders and limits, but it's impossible to define where *you* begin and end.

How about perceiving thoughts? Thoughts may be the most common thing confused with reality and a sense of self. Where are thoughts initiated? The quickest answer, of course, is "in the head", or if you're a more sophisticated thinker, your answer might be broader: "in the body". However, can you verify a thought is created in the head? How about in the body? Can you prove that 'you' are the creator of 'your' thoughts? A quick reality check reveals that thoughts come to you—you do not initiate them. They happen to you. Believing that you are the initiator of your thoughts is a symptom of the false sense of self, which leads to a derivative belief that your thoughts are true. Yet, how true are your thoughts, really?

Imagine yourself walking on a grass field. Suddenly, you notice an extraordinarily beautiful flower under your feet. The flower waves gently in the light wind with all its deep red petals unfolded to enjoy the day's light. "What a beautiful flower," you think and kneel to observe it closer. "It's so red! It must be a rose." Now, is your thought about your observation actually *a flower*? Is the deep red entity in front of your eyes really *a rose*? Can you even verify that it's actually *red*? If you uttered the word 'flower', would the sound produced by your vocal cords really be the flower? Anything you think about the flower bears a similar connection to the real flower as a photograph would—your thoughts only represent something called "a flower". There's no absolute reality in representations but the representation itself. Every single thought is an entirely relative micro-reality representing your perceptions, which are also relative to the core. Where's the reality in all those layers of relativities? Thoughts easily lure you to look to the other side of a mirror to find something of value beyond the reflections. Yet, there is no other side—only you and your mirror.

Thoughts are so hazy and quick to go by that they are more like an illusion than reality. Maybe the next time you come upon a thing called "a rose", you might put your thoughts aside and cultivate the sensation of beauty that flows within the veins of your being. Really look at the intricate dance of color and form. Maybe enjoy the subtle scent of it, or even try what it feels like to touch a thing called "a rose". When was the last time you consciously touched a flower? Examined a plant with your fingertips? Put your bare hands on green grass just to find out what it felt like? Children do that quite often—express sincere interest in things with all the available senses. Where's your inner child? Is it possible to put all your knowledge aside and get to know existence for the first time ever?

Recognizing that simple sensation of beauty is one step away from unity and wholeness. Why one step away? Isn't experiencing beauty already enough? If you're aware that there's no actual 'you' recognizing the beauty, but instead, that *you are* the sensation of beauty, something absolute is simultaneously recognized. Separation disappears like it never existed at all. The false sense of you is recognized as a reflection on an impossibly thin film of a soap bubble. Paradise lost turns into echoes of something that has actually never happened in the first place. Reality unfolds within like the petals of the rose, not initiated by you or dependent on your intellect and abilities, but all by itself without any effort. You may also recognize how your river was never disconnected from the ocean. All the reflections in your hall of mirrors actually happened in the great hall of awareness. You were never incomplete and deficient but always already whole in the background, in silence.

In this great silence of existence, sincere and unconditional appreciation for *everything that exists* arises. What exists, then? Small things. Simple things. Simple sensory perceptions of a flower swaying in the gentle wind, of water dripping in the melting snow, of wind blowing through the trees' foliage, of the sun setting in brilliant hues of orange and red, of the scent of grass in sweet morning dew, of the touch of a stone's rough surface in the fingertips, of the darkness of space in the magnificent night sky, of the nocturnal silence while your family is asleep, of the glory of awakening to a new morning, of the intricate dance of communication between fellow human beings. You don't just experience it all. You *are* all that.

Nothing much is needed: stop external searching and be available for the present moment. That's your birthright and inherent attribute as a human being. Nothing or no one can take this attribute away from you, not even yourself, even though you sometimes plunge into denial and a severe case of amnesia, rolling your boulder up all kinds of hills.

It's evident that if you were not here, your experience of this all would not be. This implies that everything you experience is included in you. Whenever your false sense of self subsides, when 'you' are not here, a sensation of unity arises from beyond the noise of the world. Frequently, when you ask someone who has done a heroic act—for example, saved a life without hesitation, risking their own in the process—they do not regard their actions as anything special. "Anyone else would have done the same," they sincerely declare. All kinds of heroic acts and miracles arise when 'you' are not here, ranging from saving another life to the most subtle expression of compassion, care, and love. They are all actions included in you, yet not done by 'you'.

It's not easy to put aside the idea of 'you' who should make life worth living in every possible way. *Existing* is a compelling idea for human beings. As far as I know, a human being is the only animal capable of imagining one's own death. For example, does a squirrel think, "This is insane! What if I fall?" while jumping from one pine tree to another? I suppose this is one of the crucial aspects of why the human species has survived, even though our bodies and senses are far inferior to many other species.

On the other hand, this very same ability to imagine your own death has obviously led to a state of predicament where you're too focused on surviving and defying death. Much like our friend Sisyphus did in the myth. You try to protect the idea of 'you' in all possible situations, be it life-threatening or just some trivial affair in your daily life. Whenever negativity arises, you'd do well to ask yourself: What am I really trying to protect here? Is there anything that truly needs protection? These questions might bring forth the magnificently spacious stillness within, which leaves no room for thinking.

When there's no room for a single thought in a situation, for extreme example, a life-threatening or a life-saving one, the idea of 'you' who has to survive is entirely absent. You do what's necessary to fulfill the situation. Just like a squirrel places his paws and claws firmly on the branch when preparing for the death-defying jump, you focus entirely on the present moment, place your paws and claws firmly on the ground of being, and then wholeheartedly commence to whatever is about to emerge.

After extreme situations, you might feel ecstatic for a fleeting moment. Is the feeling produced by resolving the situation, or could it be the ecstasy of relief from the burden of 'you'? The latter is what I'd like to call an accomplishment, a success that easily outweighs any number of survivals and achievements you experience in your days. So, it's sufficient to live life one moment after another, walking through the forest paths of existence without an investment of any sense of self.

The infinite forest of existence is crowded with paths trod by all kinds of beings, old forgotten paths overgrown by the forest again, and paths yet to be created. All paths exist for their time, crossing and merging with other paths and sometimes extending a long way alone. Seasons change one after another—summer's blossoming turns into withered leaves in the autumn, and winter's cold darkness explodes into a glorious spring awakening. A certain hint of monotony can be observed if you're aware enough. However, the closest approximation of reality is still the present moment, devoid of all paths and ideas of time. Yet another paradox in the berry bucket of existence!

As the seasons change, you can't explicitly define the essence of a tree by its appearance or the way it moves and swishes in the wind. Is a tree more a tree when it's blossoming with green leaves or covered in thick frost? Is a tree more attuned with life while sprouting with new leaves or standing motionless on a bed of withering yellow leaves? All attempts at defining a tree are just as wrong and right. How about trying to define the path? Is the path more of a path when it's easy to tread? Is it more of a path only if it leads to a destination? Any efforts in defining the path tend to lead your awareness away from the beautiful forest around you.

A life spent trying to define the trees in the forest or find meaning and purpose for 'your' path seems to be "a tale told by an idiot, full of sound and fury, signifying nothing," as Shakespeare put it. All that sound and fury reflects the mother of desires: to arrive at a blissful destination, regain a paradise lost and salvation in wholeness. There's so much smoke around this desire that it's difficult to see the fire—the false sense of self. When the fire is seen, the stillness of the forest entwines with your being, and the clarity of wisdom guides your step here and now. In this very step, which *is* the present moment, you'll find all realities.

A short merging of the twentieth century's spiritual shaker Jiddu Krishnamurti with A Course in Miracles clearly defines this:

"Nothing real can be protected
because nothing real is threatened,
and nothing unreal exists."

It's time to drop your belief that the unreal is real. What is unreal, then? That's for you to find out all by yourself. No one or nothing else can give you reality. At best, books like this, teachings like that, or people like so can *initiate* your own inquiry into reality.

You'd do well to start with a small hint though: a lot of unreality emerges within your personal perception of the world. It's up to you exclusively to unravel all unrealities. The nature of unrealities is always a maze of unnecessary information. You can't storm out of that maze by adding more layers of unrealities but by recognizing those that uphold the walls. With this simple recognition, the walls crumble down by themselves due to their own impossibility. The false sense of you that has chased all those unrealities, seeking the way out of the maze it produced itself, withdraws back into the great silence from which it emerged in the first place.

When the walls go down, you might realize that the world is coming from nowhere, and it's going to nowhere. Paths extend to infinities, and soap bubbles (dis)appear for eternities. Reality has no conceivable material, mental, or spiritual attributes whatsoever. Reality *is*. So, there's absolutely nothing to do or achieve but to give earnest attention to the present moment. That's where you witness the underlying nature of all relative realities and touch something utterly and thoroughly absolute.

What's left to do in such a world where paradises are no longer lost, and you're done chasing rainbows' ends? Only one all-encompassing purpose remains within the heart of the eternal present moment.

Be kind.

www.ingramcontent.com/pod-product-compliance
Lightning Source LLC
LaVergne TN
LVHW091612170726

843492LV00007B/2365